MY FIRST COMMUNION

Coloring & Activity Book

This Book Belongs to...

_____

My First Holy Communion Day

Date: _____

At this Holy Place:_____

Given by:_____

The People who Celebrated with me:_____

_____

I Wore:_____

My Favorite Part of the day was:_____

_____

And he took bread, gave thanks
and broke it, and gave it to them, saying,
"This is my body given for you;
do this in remembrance of me."
Luke 22:19

CONNECT THE WORD TO ITS PICTURE

CHALICE

DOVE

CROSS

CANDLE

LAMB

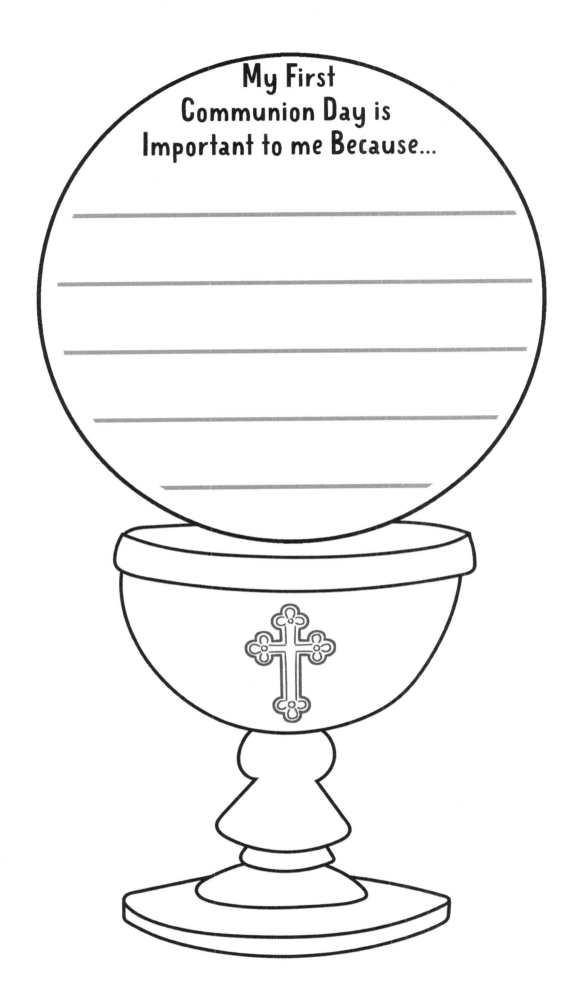

My First
Communion Day is
Important to me Because...

Who Helped Me Prepare For My First Communion?

WORD SEARCH

```
V Q C H U R C H B G
E C D C Q R P B B O
B U O Y H M A N O D
J R C M E A W I N E
E H E H M N L G N Y
S O L A A U Q I E G
U L H L D R N G C M
S Y J S K D I I G E
L M B V Y N B S O C
S A C R A M E N T N
```

GOD
SACRAMENT
CHURCH
HOLY

JESUS
BREAD
WINE

CHALICE
EUCHARIST
COMMUNION

THIS IS ME ON MY SPECIAL DAY!

I Praise God For:

My Prayers

Answered Prayers:

I'm Sorry For:

My Prayer Request:

Dear God,_____

_____

_____

_____

_____

_____

Love,_____

FIT THE WORDS INTO THE PUZZLE

I

H   H

U

C   C

R   D

S

C   N   T

CHALICE   JESUS   SACRAMENT
EUCHARIST   BREAD   CHURCH
COMMUNION   WINE   HOLY

COLOR BY NUMBER

1 - YELLOW   2 - ORANGE   3 - RED
4 - GREEN   5 - BLUE

WE LOVE HIM BECAUSE HE FIRST LOVED US!

CONNECT THE WORD TO ITS PICTURE

BREAD

BIBLE

CHURCH

JESUS

PRAYER

CROSS MAZE

START

FINISH

My Prayers

I Praise God For:

Answered Prayers:

I'm Sorry For:

My Prayer Request:

Be strong and courageous... for the Lord your God is with you wherever you go.
Joshua 1:9

Can you spot 5 differences?

MY PRAYERS

I'M GRATEFUL FOR:

I'M SORRY FOR:

CAN YOU PLEASE?

BUBBLES!

ANSWER KEY

CROSS MAZE

WORD SEARCH

```
V Q C H U R C H B G
E C D C Q R P B B O
B U O Y H M A N O D
J R C M E A W I N E
E H E H M N L G N Y
S O L A A U Q I E G
U L H L D R N G C M
S Y J S K D I I G E
L M B V Y N B S O C
S A C R A M E N T N
```

GOD
SACRAMENT
CHURCH
HOLY

JESUS
BREAD
WINE

CHALICE
EUCHARIST
COMMUNION

START

FINISH

Can you spot 5 differences?

1
2
3
4
5

FIT THE WORDS INTO THE PUZZLE

```
W I N E     C H U R C H
      U     O
      C H A L I C E
      H     Y       O
      A             M
      R             M
  B R E A D         U
      I             N
      S             I
  J E S U S         O
      T             N
  S A C R A M E N T
```

LOOK FOR THESE OTHER FUN COLORING ACTIVITIES!

www.TinyExpressionsStore.com

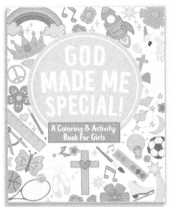
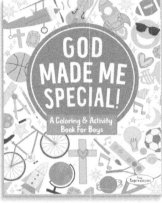

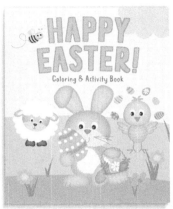

 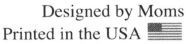

Made in the USA
Las Vegas, NV
23 April 2023